nant
gwrtheyrn
Canolfan Iaith a Threftadaeth Cymru
Welsh Language and Heritage Centre

Rebirth of the Lost Village
by Dr Carl Clowes

nant
gwrtheyrn
Canolfan Iaith a Threftadaeth Cymru
Welsh Language and Heritage Centre

Published by Ymddiriedolaeth Nant Gwrtheyrn
Charity number 1078543

ISBN: 978-0-9560072-0-9

Ymddiriedolaeth Nant Gwrtheyrn, Llithfaen, Pwllheli, Gwynedd LL53 6PA
Tel: 01758 750334   Email: post@nantgwrtheyrn.org
Website: www.nantgwrtheyrn.org

Design & Production by Jonathan Briggs at
Magic Bean Publishing, Design & Event Services
Tel: 0870 850 2125   Email: jonathan@magic-bean.co.uk
Website: www.magic-bean.co.uk

Printed & Bound by Cambrian Printers, Aberystwyth

Dedication
To the communities, past and present,
who have lived, worked and breathed life
into this remarkable valley.

Other books by the author

Antur Aelhaearn – the UK's first community co-operative Cyhoeddiadau Mei 1982
Nant Gwrtheyrn – a handbook in Welsh Y Lolfa 2004

Contents

Delivering a volume on Nant Gwrtheyrn is indeed a privilege but it creates a particular problem for me! Having relied on many people from all walks of life and all parts of Wales to bring the original vision for Nant Gwrtheyrn to reality, where does one draw the line when offering thanks for such selfless support?

Allow me then to thank in general, but nevertheless, very sincere terms those who have been of help in whatever way in their contribution to the future of this strangely haunting and yet blessed corner of Wales. The support from the Welsh community was always an inspiration. From the outset, the Trustees, the early tutors and the fund raisers all worked voluntarily to secure the future of 'Nant'. The latter number thousands, many of whom I have never met but my appreciation is total for their efforts without which we would never have succeeded. Thank you equally to the public sector, agencies, private companies and the Welsh Assembly Government for their generous support which has enriched the work and encouraged us at every stage. Not least, my thanks to the dedication of those staff who have responded to the direction and, at times, dare I say the whim of Nant's Trustees, so ensuring the developments we witness today.

Specifically, in relation to this guidebook, I am indebted to some of the historical background I have gleaned from the work of the late Prof Bedwyr Lewis Jones and Elen Rhys in their short paper *Nant Gwrtheyrn: yr hanes a'r stori* and to discussions with the local historian, the late Ioan Mai Evans. The poetic contributions from RJ Rowlands, Meirion MacIntyre Huws and RS Thomas say more than my words about the iconic nature of 'Nant' today and I am indebted for the opportunity to reflect on their interpretation of the significance of 'Nant' in contemporary Welsh life. The many historical images that are included to illustrate the past are from my personal collection but these are greatly enriched in their juxtaposition with the inspired photography of Glyn Davies, the photo-artist to whom I am indebted for his co-operation and encouragement.

Introduction

n many ways Nant Gwrtheyrn represents a microcosm of Wales itself: an agricultural background, the advent of heavy industry, its many legends, an environment second-to-none, in-migration and the influence of the Welsh language and heritage. Everything in other words which makes Wales an interesting and stimulating place to live in the early years of the second millennium.

Nant Gwrtheyrn has a particular place in the hearts of so many people who become intoxicated by its spirit and location and, in this volume, the reader has the opportunity to gain a better understanding of some of the features which make the 'Nant', as it is known colloquially, such a special place. The influence of the Iron Age, the presence of the Roman Empire and the establishment of King Gwrtheyrn are all testimony to the rich inheritance of this remarkable valley.

The village of Porth-y-Nant itself was built in the second half of the 19th century in order to meet the needs of the workers in the nearby quarry which provided an abundant supply of granite to pave the roads of some of Britain's major cities. More recently, the village of Porth-y-Nant has been recognised by CADW (the Welsh Assembly Government's Historic Environment Division) as a pioneering development of its period.

The fortunes of the granite industry, however, took a downward turn between the two World Wars when tarmacadam was introduced as a more appropriate surface for the discriminating demands of car-owners and the need for granite was seriously undermined. One by one, the villagers left their community and, by 1959, the village of Porth-y-Nant was finally deserted.

In 1978 the village, now in a ruinous state, was bought by a charitable trust, Ymddiriedolaeth Nant Gwrtheyrn, and slowly but surely, the houses were restored and 'Nant' was developed as a centre for learning Welsh. In doing so, one of the most stimulating and romantic stories of 20th century Wales unfolded as the nation united in its efforts to create the treasure we see

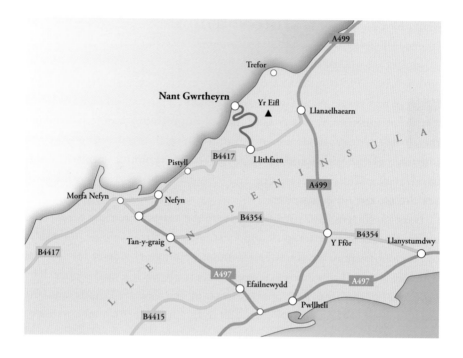

in Nant Gwrtheyrn today. It has been a long and noble struggle over 30 years and more and the job is still in hand!

For the children of Wales, the 'Nant' is famous for its legends. Is there a valley anywhere in Wales with a greater wealth of stories to tell? Rhys and Meinir, the Curse of the Three Monks, Elis Bach, the German Spy, the Eagle and Baby – not to mention Gwrtheyrn's castle and the novel *Eluned Bengoch*, based in the valley and known to so many school children.

There can hardly be another place in Wales where the combination of mountain, sea and land sit so close to one another. This closeness of the three creates a special atmosphere in the valley. It also creates an environment suitable for a wide variety of fauna, rare birds and unusual plant life and, not surprisingly as a result, several Sites of Special Scientific Interest (SSSIs) have been designated in the area.

By now, some 25,000 people from 27 different countries have had the opportunity to stay in the village and sample the Welsh language and culture.

Many have succeeded in 'crossing the bridge' and becoming fluent in the language, helping them to accomplish much in Welsh society. Gradually, the unstinting co-operation of the voluntary, public and private sectors has ensured that the 'Nant' has secured its twin objectives of promoting the language and securing employment in the area.

At the same time, the way that the Trustees have consistently ensured that the environmental agenda encompassed not only the physical, but also the linguistic, economic and social environments is well and truly established and has led to awards at a British level from the Royal Institute of British Architects, *The Times* and Shell for its inclusive vision.

In this volume, you will get a taste of the past in addition to a deeper appreciation of some of Nant's features today. Much has already been achieved in Nant Gwrtheyrn, but many more opportunities eagerly await!

The Early History
of Nant Gwrtheyrn

lthough the agricultural background of the area is predominant as one drives through the area today, there is a supply of minerals found in Bro'r Eifl that have enabled local communities survive and develop over the centuries. In addition to the plentiful supply of granite, limited quantities of iron and manganese have also been mined locally. The iron was clearly an important resource for the production of arms for the kings of the Iron Age and there is evidence that a road network was developed around the 4th century to carry the metal to the midlands of Wales and beyond. Even the Mabinogion relate the tale of Elen, friend of the Roman Emperor Magnus Maximus, persuading him to build a new road to carry metal from the area.

The best evidence of a community living in the area in the Iron Age however is Tre'r Ceiri, the fort on top of one of the peaks of Yr Eifl. Here, as many as 160 round huts are to be found in one of the largest and most dramatic forts of its kind anywhere in the British Isles. It is thought that the huts were occupied in the period 400 – 150 BC. In the 1920s a Celtic brooch, considered to be one of the largest of its period, was found on Tre'r Ceiri and the brooch is now kept in the British Museum in London.

On their departure, the Romans left their local 'stewards' behind, the Gwrtheyrnion, to rule the area. One of the most unfortunate characters of this period was Gwrtheyrn Gwrthenau of Kent. He ruled as king over the British Isles and, legend has it, he stormed on to the throne as a vicious leader. Frequently the worse for drink, it was only a matter of time before he became regarded as a fool and attempts were made to dispossess him of his throne. Because of the divisions amongst his people, he employed soldiers from Saxony to enable him to retain power. Amongst the Saxons were two brothers Hors and Hengist who, seeking more authority, invited many of their countrymen to join them. Amongst the newcomers was Hengist's daughter, Rhonwen, an irresistible temptation for Gwrtheyrn who decided he wanted to marry her. Hengist arranged a supper for Gwrtheyrn and his fellow Britons and seated his soldiers alternately with the locals only to see the soldiers arise as one and attack the Britons in the middle of the meal. Gwrtheyrn escaped with his family, firstly to Eryri and then to Nant Gwrtheyrn.

The Saxons succeeded in conquering large parts of Britain, leaving Wales and Cornwall as isolated and separate units and, for many, Gwrtheyrn remains a vivid memory of someone who betrayed his fellow Britons by employing Saxon soldiers.

It is difficult to imagine today that Nant Gwrtheyrn was well established on one of the main thoroughfares of the Middle Ages, with the mother church of the peninsula only six miles away at Clynnog Fawr. Here was the starting point for the 'Pilgrim's Trail' to Ynys Enlli (Bardsey Island). As three visits to Enlli equated with one to Rome, there was much travel along the northern coast of the peninsula. Today it is possible to walk the Pilgrim's Trail and visit three churches within reach of 'Nant' as they surround the foot of Yr Eifl – Llanaelhaearn, Carnguwch and Pistyll. In the graveyard at Llanaelhaearn there is a stone inscribed in Latin from the 6th century: 'Aliortus Elmetico Hic Iacet' (Here lies Aliortus of Elmet) whilst in Pistyll one can find a very distinct font with Celtic carvings. In Pistyll also, one can see the narrow slit for a window where those suffering from leprosy would receive their service so avoiding any contact and possible infection for other members of the public. On a more contemporary note the burial place of Rupert Davies, who acted the part of Maigret for many years in the television series, remains a popular destination for many visitors to Pistyll churchyard.

Nant Gwrtheyrn – circa 1968

Legends Abound

Gwrtheyrn

he history of Gwrtheyrn following his escape from Kent is full of adventure! Legend has it that travelling north, he was able to establish a new lineage of kings in Powys. On his way through Eryri, however, he tried to build a new fort with little success. Emrys, a young boy from the area, called to see him and told him how the lake underneath the foundations was causing the repeated collapse of the fort. Emrys went on to explain how beneath the lake there were two dragons – the red dragon of Wales and the white dragon of the Saxons – who were in constant battle with one another. Gwrtheyrn decided to free them from their underground cavern only to witness the fight continue before his eyes until the red dragon emerged victorious. It needs little imagination to see why the success of the red dragon led to it becoming the powerful symbol of Welsh nationhood today! To thank him for his help, Gwrtheyrn gave the young man a lake, Llyn Emrys and the fort, Dinas Emrys near Beddgelert.

But why venture as far as Nant Gwrtheyrn? One wonders if the rich source of iron in the area might have tempted him as it did the Romans and the Celts previously. It certainly would have been an important resource if he was to continue in battle. He was supposedly led to the area by his druids and *Historia Brittonum Nennius* refers to his arrival with them at 'Guunnessi'. According to the late Prof Melville Richards, it is possible to see an adapted version of the placename today in a farm called Gwynnys, near Pistyll.

What became of Gwrtheyrn after his arrival in the area? There are several versions of the legend. The generally accepted belief is that he built a 'castle' in the valley of Nant Gwrtheyrn. Indeed, in the 1870s, Thomas Pennant in his book *Tours of Wales* refers to the existence of a 'carnedd' or tumulus near the cliffs until about 1700. This was thought to be a grave buried under a mound of earth and, according to Pennant, when the villagers opened the grave they found a stone coffin containing the bones of a very tall man.

On early Ordnance maps of the area, Castell Gwrtheyrn is the name given to the tumulus.

According to one story, God sent fire from Heaven to burn Gwrtheyrn during a storm only for him to be killed, together with his son Gwrthefyr, whilst escaping from Garmon – one of the local leaders. In another story, Gwrtheyrn's enemies succeeded in finding him in his hiding place and he was forced to escape once again. This time, however, he was caught, killed and buried in the 'Nant'. Yet another version has it that Gwrtheyrn broke his heart after betraying the Britons and subsequently walked the mountains in a permanent stupor until he died.

Whichever version one wants to choose, it is difficult to believe there is no basis for the existence of Gwrtheyrn in the valley. However, although his name has been associated with the area for centuries, some would argue that because of the man's stupidity and betrayal of his people, the valley should be renamed.

Ioan Mai Evans, the late historian with his roots deeply entrenched in the 'Nant', argued for changing the name to Nant Llywelyn as the valley had been part of the estate of Llywelyn, the last indigenous Prince of Wales in the 13th century when he fought for the Welsh people against Edward I.

The Three Curses

A few years after the death of Gwrtheyrn, three monks called in at the 'Nant' on their pilgrimage to Enlli. Their mission was to establish a church in the valley but they received less than a welcome from the residents who rose as one against the monks and chased them from the area.

Unhappy with their rejection, the monks cast three curses on the village:

* no land in the 'Nant' would ever be sacred and nobody would ever be buried in the valley;
* 'Nant' would succeed three times and fail three times before finally failing permanently; and
* no two people from the same family in the 'Nant' would marry one another, although this was a regular happening at this period.

The night after the monks had cursed the 'Nant', a gigantic storm hit the area when the men were out fishing at sea. Every one of them drowned and, with no men left in the valley, all the women moved away, leaving Nant Gwrtheyrn without its population.

Perhaps this legend owes more to the propaganda of the Catholic church at the time which was anxious to undermine the paganism of the Celtic Church that ruled the area. Nevertheless, it is interesting to note that nobody to the best of our knowledge has been buried in the valley since then!

Even when the village was in its prime at the end of the 19th century, the villagers were not buried there. Everyone was hauled up the steep sides of the valley on a sled by some 20 quarrymen with the help of the ropes they used every day to climb the rock faces in their work. Many were buried in Llithfaen, others in nearby Pistyll.

Rhys a Meinir

The story of Rhys and Meinir is probably the most famous love story in the Welsh language. There were three farms in Nant Gwrtheyrn prior to the development of the quarries and their remains are to be seen in the valley today: Ty Uchaf, Ty Canol and Ty Hen.

About four centuries ago Rhys Maredudd, an orphaned boy, lived on one of the farms with his sister. On an adjacent farm, Meinir Maredudd lived with her father. Not surprisingly, Rhys and Meinir were playmates as children and knew one another well. In reality they were cousins but, having fallen in love, nothing would prevent them from marrying one another and this in spite of the curse of the monks. Ifan Cilia was only too happy to spread the glad news to the area, announcing the wedding date for the service in Clynnog Fawr.

The night before the wedding, as was the tradition, everybody flocked to the 'Nant' to give their wedding gifts to the happy couple: there were many small gifts and useful items such as tweed and foodstuffs for Rhys and Meinir to use after their wedding. The following morning, the mood of the villagers was a happy one as they gathered in Clynnog Fawr awaiting the arrival of the bride. The tradition at the time was for the bride to hide and the prospective groom with his friends would search for her and bring her to the church on horseback. When she saw them coming, Meinir went off to hide but, no matter how hard Rhys and his helpers searched, Meinir was nowhere to be found. Rhys, not wanting to delay proceedings, decided she had probably outwitted them and escaped to Clynnog without them seeing her. They decided to return to the church but to their great disappointment, when they arrived, she wasn't there either. As everybody was now very concerned, Rhys returned to Nant Gwrtheyrn but, searching high and low once again, nowhere was Meinir to be seen. It was obvious by the Sunday that something serious had happened to Meinir but Rhys refused to give up the search. He searched unremittingly for days, weeks and ultimately months until finally his quest led him to madness.

Every day, he would wander to an old oak tree on the cliff top where he and Meinir would go when courting and he would be heard shouting into the distance 'Meinir, Meinir!'. One night some years later, he went to shelter from a storm under the old oak when lightning struck the tree and split it in two. Inside the hollow trunk, to his disbelief he saw the remains of Meinir's wedding frock and the skeleton of his loved one. Meinir had obviously climbed into the hollow tree to hide, only to fall to its bottom and failed to climb out. The trauma was all too much for Rhys and he died on the spot. The two were buried together but, once again, the curse of the monks had struck!

Rhys and Margaret

The story of Rhys and Meinir was first seen in Welsh in a volume titled *Cymru Fu*, a collection of folk tales and legends published in October 1862. An English version, however, had been previously published in 1831 in the *Cambrian Quarterly Magazine* under the title 'The Bride of Nant Gwrtheyrn'.

In this version, the young couple were Rees and Margaret and it contained many more gory facts. This time the story refers to a fisherman at sea on a moonlit night, witnessing a skeleton walking the beach below the 'Nant'.

It describes how the local people saw two ghosts walking the shore hand in hand – the man with a beard and long hair whilst the girl had empty sockets for eyes. According to the English version, only the owl and the cormorant now land on the tree where the girl died. Perhaps the truth lies somewhere between the two versions!

Elis Bach

Elis Bach was born in 1794 in a cottage on land belonging to Ty Uchaf where he lived with his brother Robin. Although a healthy eater, always clearing his plate, it became obvious by he was aged seven that Elis was to be a dwarf. He grew little after that age and became known as Elis Bach. As a child, word has it, that on the steep inclines around the valley, his backside would hit the ground as he moved around. He may have been short but nobody could beat him as he climbed in the 'Nant'. He disliked seeing any strangers around the place and, when he saw them, he would often hide and shout at them from his 'chamber'. Unable to pronounce his words clearly, people found it difficult to understand him and he developed some strange idioms, for example 'bwyta hyn, bwyta'r cwbl o'r bin' (literally, 'eat this, eat everything from the bin').

In Elis Bach's time, a market was held in the 'Nant' with farmers from near and far attending. Each evening before the ensuing market, Elis' work involved gathering all the sheep with his three-legged sheepdog Meg. Whilst Elis was hard at work, his mother would be gathering sufficient peat for the fires, fetching water from the well and baking bread for all the visitors that would be buying and selling.

On the morning of one particular market day, two strangers had been spotted buying a lot of stock and offering over the odds for them. This was a puzzle for everyone and when the strangers went to Elis' home for some of his mother's food, he hid in one of the cupboards in the kitchen dresser. From there he could hear the two men conspiring to steal the sheep and escape with them without payment. After paying Elis' mother a small sum for the food, and only for the food, the two attempted to escape up the corkscrew road with the sheep but Elis was ready for them. He took a short cut through the woods and, able to beat them and the sheep up the track, was ready for them at the top of the 'Nant'. Having pulled a gate across the road he was, with the help of Meg, able to chase the sheep back into the woods. The two strangers recognised they had met their match and fled over Foel Gwynnus for Pistyll. That night, Meg had a supper to remember – bread, meat and milk – and the people of the area still remember the day that Elis Bach defeated the thieves. Elis Bach's field is to be seen to this day and the old ruin where he lived remains. There is a belief that there was an ancient church near Elis' cottage but, to date, it has been difficult to confirm this.

The German Spy

In the 1940s, a Mrs Margaret Fisher caused a stir when she moved to an isolated bungalow 'The Four Winds' above Carreg y Llam, on the western side of the 'Nant'. She moved to the area from Beddgelert together with 'four large hairy dogs, a cat, spinning wheel and violin' but why move to such an isolated spot?

Everybody 'knew' that she, or perhaps 'he' – as most of the local women believed – was a German spy and what better place to come to spy. There were no neighbours to keep an eye on you and from here one could flash signals unimpeded to the enemy's boats in the bay below. It was also an ideal location for the enemy's boats to dock on the quay in Carreg y Llam, to unload any personnel or help others to escape.

Then, in the small hours of one Sunday morning in February 1943, the coastguards at Porthdinllaen saw a fire on the mountain at Bwlch, Llithfaen. The wooden structure of 'The Four Winds' had burnt to the ground and the following morning, the remains of a charred body and the dogs were found. But this was not the end of the story. It had been a perfect evening with every sound carrying for miles. It was somewhat strange then that no one had heard any of the dogs barking as the house burnt. The tide had been perfect and local legend has it that Margaret Fisher escaped that night on an enemy submarine. An inquest confirmed that Mrs Fisher was a widow, her husband Captain Fisher a member of the Royal Navy, having pre-deceased her. Her only son, Lt Commander Thomas Fisher had been killed in Singapore and therefore, conveniently, nobody was able to identify whether the body was Mrs Fisher's or not.

When she lived in Beddgelert, she had supposedly been visited by Goering and previously she was said to have been educated in Prague. One wonders how much truth there is in the story. The imagination can become very vivid at such times and the mystery remains!

The Eagle and the Baby

The story that follows comes (via translation) from a script written by someone who lived in the 'Nant' at the turn of the 19th century. The date of the script is 1967 but, unfortunately, the origin remains anonymous.

'At one time, there were many eagles on the rock faces of Nant Gwrtheyrn nesting and raising their young. Although they have long since disappeared, the history of a young mother on one splendid summer's day is now part of 'Nant's legend. She lived in a cottage at the foot of the 'Nant' where one day she was outside doing the washing and had taken the baby's cot outside to be with her. Her baby was fast asleep in the quietness that pervaded the valley that day as she went to the house for a moment. Then, in disbelief, the mother heard the sound of wings and, as she rushed out, saw to her horror, a large eagle with her baby in its talons flying off towards its nest on the rocks. Her cries echoing around the cliffs fetched a number of strong quarrymen running to her help but the steepness of the cliffs made it impossible for them to reach the nest and they had to abandon their attempts. The mother, still not despairing, ran to find a rope, climbed the steep face herself and, finally, reached the eagle's nest. There, to her delight, she was able to rescue her baby

*who was still alive, before carrying the little one down to the bottom
under her arm. Who can measure the love and joy of a mother? The
love of a mother overcomes all difficulties.'*

Luned Bengoch

This novel by Elizabeth Watkin-Jones, is located in Nant Gwrtheyrn and the
surrounding area in the 15th century. For many of Wales' children who have
read the book, it has immortalised Nant Gwrtheyrn. It follows the fortunes of
Glyndwr and his attempts to free Wales from its oppressors. One of the most
ardent supporters of the prince in the novel is Rhys, the son of Huw Fychan,
who lived in Castell Nant Gwrtheyrn. He, together with his friend Luned, an
adventurous red-head, come face to face with numerous dangers in their
attempts to get a message to Glyndwr in Pumlumon whilst Luned fights
against Merfyn Goch, one of the area's biggest and most cruel scoundrels.

The old ruined byre (below left) – now Caffi Meinir

Sunset at Caffi Meinir, 2008

Development of
Porth-y-Nant

t their peak, the granite quarries of Yr Eifl were amongst the biggest in the world for creating setts, the name given to the stone shaped into various sizes but most commonly found as cubes some 15 to 20 cms in size. They were used for surfacing the roads and pavements of major cities in England as the major industrial centres developed. The particularly hard quality of the granite made it ideal for the hooves of horses needing a good grip.

Work began in the 'Nant' in 1851, almost 20 years after the opening of the quarries in Trefor and the 'Gwyliwr' near Nefyn. Until then, the three farms Ty Uchaf, Ty Canol and Ty Hen had been the mainstay of the valley, rearing cattle and some 500 sheep annually. With its shelter between the mountains and sea, the land was particularly productive. It was very fertile

The drag cart traditionally used for transporting goods

and considered a special place for early produce. The call of the shepherd and the sound of their accompanying sheep was, for the most part, all that broke the silence and the busiest week of the year was shearing time.

Today, goats from Nant Gwrtheyrn are traditionlly chosen to lead the Welsh Fusiliers but, historically, goats were gathered off the mountains, some being slaughtered to provide meat for the winter. This was a tough and very red meat that would be put into tubs and heavily salted. A heavy weight was then placed on top of the meat for some months to make it more tender.

The valley, however, was to be transformed by the development of the quarry. The first quarry owner was Hugh Owen from Ynys Môn who soon sold the quarry on to a Mr Dodd and so began the work of building 13 small houses, or barracks, to accommodate the workers. His tenure was also relatively short-lived and it fell to a new owner, Mr Benthol, to finish the work on the barracks. The remains of the barracks can still be seen to this day just beyond Ty Hen. From 1861, a Liverpool company Kneeshaw and Lupton

Feral goats with young in Nant Gwrtheyrn

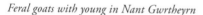

began to develop the 'Nant' further and over the next 40 years there were major developments.

People moved to the area on a big scale. Many came from Penmaenmawr and Llanfairfechan as settsmen and 'greigwyr' (workers on the rock face) and many of the early workers came from Ireland. Their role was to crush the 'metlin' as they had no particular skill for sett making. Soon the number of local Welshmen working there also increased as they moved from the relatively poor agricultural holdings in the area to the much higher paid work in the quarry. There was an equal flow of settsmen from England, notably Leicestershire where there was a quarrying tradition and the required skills were available. The names of these settlers are to be seen and heard in the area to this day – Bracegirdle, Cullen, Baum etc, – each and every one now thoroughly Welsh in their language and culture! The demand for granite increased phenomenonally in the second half of the 19th century and, by 1890, there were three major quarries in the valley: Cae'r Nant, Porth-y-Nant and Carreg y Llam.

Industrial relics remain as a stark reminder of the past history

This had an inevitable impact on the population. Where previously there were just three farms and some 16 people living in the valley, now the barracks also became too small to accommodate the newcomers and in 1878 the company decided to build 26 new houses and call the development 'Port Nant'. These are the houses that can be seen in the village to this day with the terraces referred to initially as 'Mountain View' and 'Sea View' but now, reflecting the role of the centre, more appropriately named 'Trem y Mynydd' and 'Trem y Mor'. There was a village shop run co-operatively alongside the village's bakehouse located at the end of Trem y Mynydd across fom the chapel. Here the common currency was the co-operative's own coinage minted especially for this isolated community and reflecting its self-supportive nature.

At the lower end of the village below Trem y Mynydd the Plas, a substantial mansion house was built. Here the quarry manager 'lived like a king' according to one of the former residents. His house was isolated from the rest of the village by a high wall which afforded a separate access. It remained this way until the 1980s when the current Trust created the opening to facilitate ease of access from the village to the Plas.

In an industry where injuries were frequent and there were no sickness or disability payments, the workers inventiveness led them to create their own 'insurance' scheme. Dr Huw T Edwards, the union leader, describes how his father was seriously injured on the quarry face whilst still a young man and unable to work for some time. As a result, the quarrymen, including many of the Irish immigrants, made a collection every other Saturday night for nine months so that his father had a living wage.

In the bay below Nant Gwrtheyrn, three landing 'stages' were built to enable boats to load their cargoes of granite with each quarry having its own 'stage'. Not surprisingly, having delivered their loads the boats would return to Nant Gwrtheyrn with some of the goods found in the 'exotic' locations of Birkenhead and Liverpool, many of the latest fashions being introduced to the 'Nant' long before they were seen elsewhere on the peninsula! This was also how the first fuel cargoes arrived in the area, with coal being transported from the English cities. Prior to that, fuel was limited to the burning of brushwood and wood collected locally although the late Margaret Jones, Glanrhyd,

Above: Trem y Mynydd in ruins, 1976

Above: Y Plas, the former manager's house, facing demolition

Llanaelhaearn who lived as a child in the village, related to me how they would also use dried cow dung as a fuel for heating and cooking.

Boats up to 200 tons were able to dock safely in the bay and the quarry owners invested in four such craft to carry the 'metlin' to the major English towns – the 'Tolfaen', 'Sylfaen', 'Gwynfaen' and 'Calchfaen'. The Tolfaen sank off the coast of Ynys Môn with the loss of all the crew. Sylfaen was also lost, this time in the nearby bay at Porthdinllaen, but with a happier ending as all the crew were saved.

One stormy night, another boat, the 'Amy Summerfield', got into difficulty whilst docking at the Cae'r Nant stage. Having secured the bow, the storm took hold of the rest of the boat and whipped it on to the beach, entangling the propellor in the rocks, leaving the vessel to face the worst elements of the storm. The boat was wrecked and some of the remains can still be seen. The stage survived that night but was finally brought down in a storm in the 1980s and, again, some of the remnants can still be seen.

The quarries reached their peak towards the end of the 1880s and by the Census of 1886 the total population of the valley had increased considerably from the three farming families that originally lived there. Now, there were an additional 190 quarrymen and their families.

When the industry was in its prime, Saturday night presented a 'special' opportunity for the quarrymen to relax as this was the night when the Irish would gather in the Victoria Hotel, now 'Y Fic'. According to one witness at the time 'the village went wild and we as children used to make sure we were home before the Hotel was closed. The arguments and fighting amongst the revellers used to frighten us as children. Some would finish up sleeping on the "corkscrew" road on the way home and be found the following morning.'

The old 'corkscrew' road in 1982

One of the corners on the road down to 'Nant' is named after such an incident. It was a stormy night with strong winds drifting the heavy snow when a Mrs Butler, much worse for the drink, fell into a drift on her way home where, unable to get up, she remained until the following morning. That day, her husband began searching for her with some of the villagers only to find her dead on the turning known to this day as 'tro Mrs Butler' (Mrs Butler's turning).

Religion in the Nant

In the early days of development of the quarry, few of the villagers in Port Nant would venture to Llithfaen for the Sunday service and, as a result, services were held initially in an old wooden shack – 'y Babell Goed' just above Ty Hen. 'Nant' was a very austere place to live with the barracks offering little by way of comfort. According to one historian, this led to the workers living a life of 'revelling and drunkenness' for much of their time. A Minister from Llithfaen would visit each Sunday, and a Catholic priest on alternate Mondays,

The magic of Capel Seilo at night

New life: Capel Seilo – 1968 and 2008

in an attempt to moderate the excessive lifestyle of the residents. Then in 1875, the church came under the care of the Calvinistic Methodists who built Capel Seilo at a cost of £300, so providing a new purpose-built chapel for worship with seating for 130. Interestingly, this became the first 'English cause' in the Llŷn peninsula, presenting more than a little irony for the modern-day user! At the turn of the 19th century, there was a membership of 40 in the chapel with an additional 60 children attending Sunday school and the 'Nant' was felt to be worthy of its own Minister. Unfortunately, none remained very long and the last Minister, the Rev GW Jones of Parc, Ynys Môn left in 1914. The old wooden chapel became a victim of yet another storm although its foundations were to be seen until some landscaping work hid them in the early 1990s. Capel Seilo, now a listed building, today acts as a limited resource for the enquiring visitor.

Education in the Nant

With an increasing number of children living in the 'Nant' by the end of the 19th century, it became imperative to provide formal education in the valley. Although the responsibility lay with the quarry company, they asked the chapel Minister to oblige and provide schooling on a daily basis, even though they rarely had any formal training to do so. In the beginning, the school was held in one of the houses in Trem y Mynydd before moving to the Babell Goed as the numbers grew. With the regular change in Ministers and, consequently, a frequent absence of any educational provision in the valley, the children would either travel to school in Llithfaen or, failing that, stay at home.

The irregularity and unsatisfactory nature of the provision was only addressed when the County Council took on the responsibility for the children's education in 1908. The situation was still not easy, however, with the migratory nature of so many of the workers creating a difficult situation for the teachers. This was of sufficient concern to His Majesty's Inspectorate of Schools that in a report of September 1910, the Inspector Lewis Jones Roberts reported 'it has not been possible to maintain consistency in the school's work and the standard of the pupils' work in the school is unacceptable'. He also suggested changing the name of the school 'from the hybrid "Port Nant" into the suggestive Nant Gwrtheyrn (sic)'. Around the same time, a new teacher with contemporary teaching methods was appointed and such was the improvement that by the next autumn, the Inspector was able to report 'there has been a substantial improvement in the general condition of the school. Particularly good lessons have been found for Recitation, Music and Nature and there has been a substantial increase in reading both in Welsh and English.'

In spite of this, around the same time, the number of children began to fall so that by 1915 there were just 17 pupils in the school. This was the consequence of the reduced demand for granite, leading to a gradual demise of the 'Nant' quarry and a fall in the village's population. Some of the workers found work in other quarries but Chwarel y Nant was never to see a similar

The way it was – looking towards Ty Hen through the windows of the threatened Plas, 1983

level of activity again. The houses began to empty one at a time only to be occupied by some of the residents from the barracks. This was to prove fortuitous as, in 1925, most of the barracks disappeared in an almighty landslide.

Chwarel y Nant was to re-open during the 1930s as the demand for hardcore to develop roads increased. This was to maintain a population sufficient to keep the chapel and school open for some years but the inevitable decline was to take its toll. Chapel members had fallen to 12 by the mid 1930s as more villagers moved away from the area or went to live in Llithfaen. Chwarel y Nant finally closed before the Second World War and the quarries of Cae'r Nant and Carreg y Llam a little later. The school closed in 1948 and all three quarries had closed by the end of the 1940s leaving an increasing number of empty properties in the village. Paradoxically people, particularly those who were homeless, found the 'Nant' an attractive option and continued to move into the area necessitating a re-opening of the school by the Education Committee in 1949. Gwen Evans, the last teacher in the school, today lives in Llithfaen.

Ultimately, there was to be no salvation for this former quarrying community and the last people moved out in 1959. Little by little, the place became overgrown becoming a perfect hideaway for an occasional tramp seeking solitude, the quiet only disturbed by the noise of the sheep and feral goats scrambling over the remains of the quarry and the high-pitched note of the chough championing one of its last bastions in the west.

Nant from 1978:
Development of the Language Centre

uch was the history of the 'Nant' until 1970 when I had the privilege of moving to the area with my family to begin work in general practice. The practice was single-handed and based in Llanaelhaearn which acted as the fulcrum for Bro'r Eifl. With 1,200 patients on the register, they would travel to see me at any one of three centres: Bryn Meddyg in Llanaelhaearn where we also lived, the chapel vestry in Maes-y-Neuadd, Trefor and the surgery I inherited in Llithfaen – a former butcher's shop, primitive in the extreme. The latter, however, no more than a corrugated iron shed, was to play a key part in the fortunes of Nant Gwrtheyrn.

Here, at the end of a Saturday morning surgery in June 1972 Mrs Knox, a Llithfaen resident and wife of a former 'Nant' quarry manager, came to see me. The normal doctor-patient discussion took its course before she let it be known that the 'Nant' was likely to be sold in the near future. She had been aware of my interest for some time previously and was obviously delighted to share the news gleaned from her husband who was now working in the Arennig quarry near Y Bala, having been transferred there following the closure of the local quarry.

I could barely contain my excitement and there was no option but to follow up this important 'lead'. At the age of 28, one can change the world! Armed with nothing more than strong conviction that something had to be done to 'save' the local communities from terminal decline, here was the opportunity to act!

But why the determination to 'save' the local communities and what exactly were my anxieties for the area? With the gradual closure of the quarries, so the population had also gone into serious decline. To put the concern into perspective, when the quarries were at their peak, some 2,000 men were employed in this heavy industry within a five-mile belt along the coast. Farming patterns had also seen a remarkable change. Prior to the second World War, many of the young men worked on the land but things were never to return to their previous pattern. Increasing mechanisation and the advent of the tractor saw to that and by the early 1970s relatively few farms employed their own labourers or farm workers. Without work, there was really no reason for families to remain and the resulting fall in population was reflected in the National Census returns. In 1921, the population of the parish of Llanaelhaearn, which included Trefor, was 1,543. By 1971, one third of the population had disappeared and it had fallen to 1,059. The parish of Pistyll, which included Llithfaen, showed a similar picture and, of course, the population of Porth-y-Nant had disappeared entirely.

The school in Llithfaen had closed in the 1960s and between 1970-1972 there had been a fierce battle to save Ysgol Llanaelhaearn from closure. This proved successful and became a catalyst for further community action. Cymdeithas y Pentrefwyr – a villagers' association – was formed and from that emerged Antur Aelhaearn, the first 'community co-operative' in the United Kingdom with a remit to secure a future for the village within the resources available. But did 'Nant' not also present many opportunities?

The area's communities were rapidly disappearing. The lack of hope for the future and the lack of confidence that that brought had a marked affect on the health of the community, something that was readily seen on the faces of those presenting in the surgery from day to day. At the same time there was little by way of answers from those who had authority. There was no alternative but once again to try and find our own solutions!

A letter to Amalgamated Roadstone Corporation, the owners of Porth y Nant followed, enquiring as to when they would be selling the village. Initially, there was a somewhat non-committal reply. Then, I recall the day I shot into the drive at Bryn Meddyg in my old VW 'beetle'. It was a Tuesday morning in the summer of 1972 following another surgery in Llithfaen and once more Mrs Knox provided the excitement. This time it was the news that things appeared to be moving 'seriously'. Once in the house, I was on the phone immediately with Amalgamated Roadstone and speaking authoritatively on behalf of an aspiring 'Nant Gwrtheyrn Trust', persuading them of our genuine wish and intention to buy the village should they be in a position to sell! The response was encouraging. There was to be a 'decision within three weeks or so and the likely cost was to be £35,000'.

But what to do with a deserted village – the 'ghost village' as the occasional visitor described it? I saw it as an important resource for the area, a magical place and one that had left a big impression on me when I first set eyes on it in the mid-60s. Then, the village still had an air of hope. The rooves were intact and the chapel was as if there had been a service there the previous Sunday with the hymn numbers on the display board bearing witness to the life of this once-thriving community. Now, in spite of the decline, what was important was that this gem was used for the benefit of the local population creating hope within the community and encouraging opportunities for employment in the area.

In 1967, the first Welsh Language Act was passed – an act which gave equal validity to Welsh and English in Wales for the first time. The Act was based on a report from Sir David Hughes Parry, a barrister, former Vice-Chancellor of the University of London and a son of Llanaelhaearn. The act undoubtedly helped to create a new climate with more people looking for services in

A forlorn Nant Gwrtheyrn in 1970

Welsh from public bodies and an increased pressure on those same public organisations to provide such a service. Frequently, nevertheless, despite considerable good will from the public sector it was often difficult to appoint personnel with appropriate professional qualifications who also had a knowledge of Welsh. It seemed that what was needed was a 'machine' to immerse people in the Welsh language so that they became confident Welsh speakers. Only then would we see a situation where candidates, otherwise well qualified, would no longer be unable to take up an appointment on the basis that they were lacking the necessary skills in Welsh.

Bringing the two visions together – the creation of employment on the one hand and a machine to 'Cymricise' on the other – the 'Nant' offered an unique solution and an embryonic Trust, Ymddiriedolaeth Nant Gwrtheyrn, was formed with several close allies in support to give validity to our campaign.

Unfortunately, for several years the ambition was to be painfully unfilfilled. The news that 'Nant' would be sold became public knowledge and soon became the focus of attention in some of the major English papers such as the *Guardian* and the *Sunday Times*. This inevitably created even more interest in the fate of the village and, of course, much more competition for us. Amalgamated Roadstone opened the doors to the wider market and, as a result, over 100 various parties – companies, trusts and individuals – expressed an interest in buying the place. When the people of Bro'r Eifl learnt of the true nature of the interest, there was considerable concern amongst the local community. How would they cope with a centre for drug addicts or the rehabilitation of offenders? Alternatively, the idea of a holiday camp or the intention of BP to use the valley to 'hide' the tanks thought to be required for a Celtic Sea oil bonanza?

Just when it appeared that things were moving in the right direction, there was a wholly unexpected turn of events. Two weeks before a scheduled meeting with Amalgamated Roadstone to finalise an agreement in Betws-y-Coed in 1975, we were advised that the company was to be bought by Consolidated Goldfields and that we would need to re-commence negotiations with ARC, a related company. It proved a long and hard campaign persuading ARC that they should sell to the embryonic Trust, an organisation with no obvious financial means to secure the village's future! After all, there was little we could do to compete financially with some of the big organisations interested in the 'Nant', either in terms of the initial purchase or the subsequent re-building and refurbishment of the village. And so battle commenced!

There was no alternative. Lacking in funds as we were, I wrote to several hundred supporters of the language outlining the proposal and seeking a financial pledge should the village become ours. Fortunately, there was a warm and enthusiastic response and several thousand pounds of promissory notes were forthcoming. At the same time, a massive publicity campaign was begun to make sure that the quarry owners could not ignore us. We lobbied hard for months on end and seeking support from the local councils, petitioning, writing letters to the press and so forth became an integral part of life.

After all, our thought process went, here was a company that, by virtue of its quarrying, spent most of its resources changing the face of rural Wales and despoiling the environment and, quite simply, they needed friends! With our proposed Trust being the only organisation in Wales out of the 106 that had shown interest in buying 'Nant', here was an ideal opportunity for the company to gain favour and support in Wales.

The strategy was successful and the hard work brought success as, in July 1978, in a simple ceremony in the old school in Llithfaen, Porth-y-Nant was transferred to a charitable trust now registered as Ymddiriedolaeth Nant Gwrtheyrn for the sum of £25,000. ARC were at this stage totally committed to our aims and immediately presented a gift of £5,000 to help us commence our appeal for restoration. The village, comprising of 26 houses, the Plas (manager's house), Capel Seilo (chapel), a ruined byre (now Caffi Meinir) together with approximately eight acres of land down to the high-water mark, was finally in our hands. It was some years later before Ty Canol and the forest with another 70 acres leading to the top of the cwm, and finally Ty Hen, became the property of the Trust. The relationship with the former quarry owners has continued and, as recently as 2007, a further 100 acres of Heritage Coast (Chwarel y Nant) to the west of Porth-y-Nant was transferred to the Trust by Hanson Plc for a nominal sum.

The enormity of the task ahead was difficult to overstate but the widespread support that was to ensue is a tribute to the vision of the people of Wales.

The public, private and voluntary sectors, each in their individual ways, played a role in securing a future for 'Nant'. The houses had deteriorated significantly by the beginning of the 1970s. Many had lost their rooves, all had lost their floors and windows and, not surprisingly, people were now increasingly referring to the 'Nant' as a 'ghost village'. The deterioration owed much to the elements but also the village offered a plentiful supply of repair materials for locals living in the impoverished communities of the area. An invasion of hippies added to its terminal decline and the New Atlantis Commune, as they were to be known, left its indelible mark as every material that could be used to make a fire now disappeared. The period of negotiation in the 1970s had proved to be an extremely frustrating period with each visit to the 'Nant' witnessing a further decline in what we were negotiating for and yet were helpless to do anything about! One John Lennon was to come to the rescue, whether by design or default we will never know. The local press reported that he bought an island in Clew Bay off the west coast of Ireland and, shortly after, the commune moved in its entirety – vacating Porth-y-Nant and leaving us to our own devices.

The challenge was now all ours! Not only was the village skeletal in its structure, the access to the village left a lot to be desired and there was no electricity, no sewerage system or mains water. Indeed, even at this stage, questions were raised about the legitimacy of the proposal to develop the 'Nant' and my sanity called into question by the closest of friends! Other easier alternatives for a language centre were preferred but none offered the same 'inspiration' and that from my perspective was what the language and the area needed!

And so the work began. A national appeal was launched with Lord David Davies of Llandinam as Chair. In practice, a governmental programme was particularly instrumental in enabling us to make progress. With its aim of taking the young long-term unemployed off the dole, the Manpower Services Commission (MSC) funded some of the first improvements. They paid for the salaries of the young people and gave us an additional 10% for materials. That still left a considerable shortfall and it was now that the various promises of support were to prove so helpful. Cyngor Dwyfor, the local authority in the area, was to contribute and that, together with some voluntary help, enabled us to refurbish our first property and hold the first course in the 'Nant' at Easter 1982. The resources were extremely limited and an entrepreneurial spirit ruled the air. With no mains electricity, a diesel generator was brought to the rescue. Noisy and smelly, it didn't detract from the success of the course run entirely by volunteer tutors, the late Gwenno Hywyn and Merfyn Morgan. This was our first success and 'Nant' had begun to make its bone fide mark as a Canolfan Iaith (Language Centre), a new concept but one that was to become a brand embellished in the minds of many thousands of learners over the next 30 years. At last, the 'machine' had begun to move, albeit in first gear!

The voluntary nature of the majority of the teaching continued for some time, albeit supported by a paid 'executive' from the early 1980s. A series of part-time and occasional tutors employed by the Trust ensued and it took another five years before the Centre was in a position to employ its first full-time tutor. Meic Raymant, himself a learner from south Pembrokeshire, was appointed in 1987 as 'Nant's Head Tutor and, with his commitment and

A former resident ponders on the past, 1970

leadership, the Centre was able to develop a range of courses and resources appropriate to the task. As a result, 'Nant' was able to attract learners from near and far and, during his 13-year tenure, attracted increasing numbers, broadening the appeal and bringing considerable success to the early vision. 'Nant' had now reached 'second gear'!

When the casual visitor chances on Nant Gwrtheyrn today, they will see a variety of names on the individual houses, each reflecting a sponsor's commitment; public bodies and quasi-public organisations side by side with huge support from the voluntary sector and groups of learners. The contributions and efforts from learners and volunteers were an inspiration in their own right: from gathering copper wire (with Manweb's permission!) on Yr Wyddfa – Snowdon, a sponsored race around Llyn Tegid, walking Britannia Bridge at its opening, contributions to the BBC learners' programme *Catchphrase* and so on... this money was to become the leavening in the mix with MSC support and enabled us to improve the houses slowly, one at a time,

The long haul begins as work commences

firstly those in Trem y Mynydd and then Trem y Mor. Each house developed its own character, each had an opening ceremony in recognition of the sponsor's efforts and each event added to the sense of ownership of the people of Wales in the resurrection of the village and, with it, the creation of an important resource for Wales in the work of restoring the national language to its rightful place.

Things were not always to run smoothly. The local authority, Cyngor Dosbarth Dwyfor warned of a pending demolition order on the Plas. In fairness to the authority, the arch of bricks, with no visible support, that greeted one on entry to the Plas gave them little alternative. Providence, however, was to be on our side. With time rapidly running out and our pleadings reaching the end of any reasonable stay of execution, the necessary funding to secure the future arrived by courtesy of the Welsh Office. The degree of dereliction in the Plas was daunting and the reconstruction work was urgent but no sooner had it commenced than there was to be yet another

The trustees receive a contribution towards resotoration following a national appeal in 'Y Faner' magazine!

turn of fate and work had to be put on hold! A nest of choughs, a rare and protected bird found in Nant Gwrtheyrn, had decided to locate in the Plas. This was to become the source of much dialogue between ourselves and the Welsh Office as the transfer of money from one financial year to another was an exceptional event! We succeeded, however, and on completing the restoration of the Plas, we celebrated with an international conference on Lesser Used European Languages with delegates from all over Europe. John Hume MP and the member of the European Parliament who first raised the question of official status for the lesser used languages was a guest as was the local MP, Dafydd Wigley who had raised similar issues within the UK parliament. Today, the Plas acts as the main focus for teaching in the Centre and also offers a small library and place to relax and socialise in the evening.

One of the central features of the village is the cafe which now caters not only for those on courses but also visiting groups, weddings and passing tourists. But this was not always the case. Caffi Meinir as it is today has

Young, previously unemployed, people work on restoration

gradually evolved from the ruined remnants of a former farm building. Having raised the walls to roof height, a corrugated zinc roof was the best we could manage on a limited budget. It was some years later before the building was extended and, because of the inadequacies of the road at the time, it took the support of an RAF helicopter on a training exercise from Y Fali to bring the necessary roof trusses to Porth-y-Nant to ensure the development.

The experience of the inadequacies of the road was nothing new. When Ymddiriedolaeth Nant Gwrtheyrn bought the village in 1978, the access road was unsurfaced, presented a 1:3 gradient and had been used for motor-bike trials. Commonly referred to as the 'corkscrew' road, it was totally impractical for the planned purpose of the centre. It was, however, a public road and one of the conditions established by Gwynedd County Council in giving us planning permission to develop the Centre was that we did not ask for it to be upgraded on the public purse! There was to be a period of hard bargaining when the same authority subsequently looked to close the road as a public

Constructing the new road commences

highway and transfer the responsibility to the newly-formed Trust. However, a mutual understanding was reached with Gwynedd which gave us some seed-funding to re-develop the road but the responsibility was then firmly ours!

But how to develop the road? The possibility of re-directing it and easing the gradient seemed wholly impossible to the layman's eye. It was a chance conversation with the Forestry Commission who had expressed an interest in selling their estate based on Ty Canol that opened up new opportunities. Having purchased the land, we were then in a position to seek advice as to other possibilities regarding access and, with the skills of the Forestry Commission's planning team and Jones Bros, Ruthin as contractors, we succeeded in creating a totally new road. This not only transformed the access and facilitated communication with the 'Nant' but also gave us confidence and renewed credibility for our plans for the future.

By 1990, the first round of renewal of the village was essentially complete with the houses offering a cosy and comfortable experience. A reservoir for the water supply had been created, a phone introduced and all the other 'services' were now in place. A play area for children had been created behind Trem y Mor and, with the restoration of the chapel, there was no longer a place for the sheep to hide and an annual Cymanfa Ganu (singing festival) was reinstated. We had reached the end of an important phase in 'Nant's recent history.

Nant Gwrtheyrn: an environmental treasure trove

simple description of Nant Gwrtheyrn, focusing on the social and cultural environment, can easily lose sight of the wealth of its natural environment. Earlier we had a taste of the valley's history and its legends but the physical environment can offer every bit as much interest. Denoted an Area of Outstanding Natural Beauty (AONB) and an integral part of Llŷn's Environmentally Sensitive Area (ESA), the vicinity of Nant Gwrtheyrn can also boast three Sites of Special Scientific Interest (SSSI).

Gallt y Bwlch

Standing half-way between Porth-y-Nant and Carreg y Llam and rising to some 170 metres above sea level, Gallt y Bwlch is of particular interest for its stunted oak forest where the trees grow no more than two to three metres in height. The stunted nature of the forest results from a combination of poor soil, strong winds and a constant attack from the salt of the sea. The same effect can be seen on the hazel and other bushes growing alongside and, as this is essentially a natural forest with little or no intervention by man, it has a particular significance. The area has also been identified by the European Commission as a Special Area of Conservation, notable as one of the best examples of sea-cliff vegetation in Britain.

Carreg y Llam

The cliffs of Carreg y Llam to the west of the bay are important for their colonies of sea birds, being one of the most important nesting sites in north Wales. The cliffs rise to about 100 metres and on the most inaccessible rock faces one can find breeding colonies of guillemots (some 2,000 nests) and kittiwakes (in excess of 500 nests), more than anywhere else in the region. Also, albeit in smaller numbers, auks and razorbills are found on the steeper cliffs. Other breeding species, including the fulmar, shag, cormorant and herring gull, all claim their territory on the headland and gannets pass by offshore. Reference has already been made to the importance of the chough which nests locally and which one can see and hear regularly but other birds of significance, notably the kestrel, buzzard and the peregrine falcon are also seen in and around the valley.

Below Porth-y-Nant grey seals swim in the bay and occasionally there is a glimpse of the bottlenose dolphin. This is a particular honour as these dolphins are part of only two surviving populations in the British Isles.

Native woodland below the village

Yr Eifl

Yr Eifl is the name given to the range of peaks sheltering Porth-y-Nant from the south. The range rises to 564 metres and, because of its proximity to the sea, is home to several interesting features. The flora of the slopes exhibit a transition from lowland maritime shrub heath to that of montane heath in the upper areas. Heather and bell-heather dominate the drier areas with western gorse on the lower slopes. Cowberry is found on the upper slopes and species such as butterwort and yellow sedge are also found. On the highest parts of Yr Eifl there are extensive areas of block scree with some dauntingly large boulders and scrambling to the peaks can be challenging – and dangerous – in misty conditions.

The slopes that face the sea are exceedingly steep with some vast gullied precipitous slopes reaching 300 metres above sea level at the highest point. Here one can see a number of interesting oceanic plants including the lanceolate spleenwort (Asplenium billotii) and, nearby, on both natural and man-made rock faces, the chough survives well feeding on the rich habitat of the ungrazed moorland. Regular visitors to the village are the wild goats which roam the mountain as they probably have done from the middle ages. On the scree above the village they can regularly be heard to skirmish but they no longer provide a source of food and skins for clothing as they once did!

At the top of the highest point of Yr Eifl there is a listed 'carnedd' or tumulus – one of many in the area – but for interest and its sheer scale this is outshone by Tre'r Ceiri, the splendid fort dating back to the Iron Age which rules supreme from the top of the peak furthest from the sea.

In 1960 the Forestry Commission planted some 70 acres in the valley of Nant Gwrtheyrn, predominantly lodgepole pine on the upper slopes and sitka spruce lower down. In both instances they have had the unfortunate effect of stifling most growth beneath the trees. The trees are also of little value and the terrain makes it difficult to extract them. The trustees however, would wish to gradually replace the existing plantation with more appropriate and indigenous species. Some consolation is found in a few locations, notably along the river, where there are several examples of ash and hazel surviving and in the wetter sites alder and willow can also be found.

The informed eye will also be able to spot several species of indigenous plants and flowers as one wanders around Nant Gwrtheyrn and many of these would have been used for medicinal purposes. Adjacent to the path by the chapel, for example, one can readily see wormwood, often used to treat arthritis or migraine; nearby, lesser celandine used for treating inflammation and haemorrhoids is found as is the foxglove, the source of digitalis used for treating heart conditions. The rowan tree, whose berries were used to protect the community from witchcraft, is present in the valley and also spleenwort used to feed the cattle. On the way to the beach, the dwarf thistle, parsley fern (arctic alpine), bachelor's button, wood sorrel, milkwort, tormentil and the mountain fern are all to be seen.

Walking the beach reveals its own treasures with the majority of the stones being glacial in origin and many having travelled from far and wide. Basalt and flint from the north of Ireland, pre-Cambrian green stones from across the sea on Ynys Cybi and quartz, silica, jasper and schist mica coming from more local sources around the peninsula. Mixed in with them is the local granite offering an infinite variety of interest with their spots varying in size from one stone to the next.

The area also offers a retreat for several animal species of interest. In addition to the wild goats, badgers, foxes and polecats, smaller carnivores such as the weasel and stoat are also found here. There are reports of otters and a 'large animal crossing the road high up the slopes' might, in the words of Prof Cedric Milner, Bangor University, have been a pine marten. If a marten, it would be a most important addition to the fauna of the area. Both tawny and white owls are established in Nant Gwrtheyrn as are several bat species who find refuge in the many ruins around the valley.

The environment man has created has now been recognised by CADW, the Welsh Historical Buildings organisation which, in 1999, registered Porth-y-Nant as of Grade II importance because the site represents 'Buildings of an Architectural or Historical Interest'. Trem y Mor and Trem y Mynydd, the two rows of housing for quarryworkers were very much in the vanguard of development in the 1870s. In an area where tuberculosis was rife, they offered accommodation far superior to that found elsewhere in the area. Here, replacing the cramped cottages of the quarrymen and peasant farmers, was housing with plenty of light, high ceilings and good air circulation. For the first time, the welfare of the workers was an important feature of industrial development in the area.

The Plas, the former manager's house, together with the drive leading to it has also been listed as a resource of historical significance. Originally separated from the rest of the village by a high stone wall, it is seen as an example of housing for a managing class separate from the workers and yet an integral part of the industrial development as a whole. Capel Seilo, AD1878, was the final part of the jigsaw registered by CADW – 'a simple Calvinistic Methodist chapel set on a platform levelled out of the hillside' and became an essential part of this forward-looking plan to improve the provision for the quarry workers.

Y Plas reinstated – Nant's teaching centre

The wider environment of the Welsh language

eople from far and wide with an interest in the Welsh language are attracted to Nant Gwrtheyrn. One often asks why and, invariably, the commitment that the village represents to the Welsh language and heritage is uppermost in their minds. Many have supported the project directly or indirectly in its 30-year history or are aware of the strong identity and 'brand' that Nant represents in securing a future for the language. The visitor with an interest in Welsh therefore feels 'safe' within the Centre and able to use the language without any question of feeling insecure – not, unfortunately, always the case in contemporary Wales.

In addition, Nant Gwrtheyrn is in a privileged language situation. In the communities surrounding Yr Eifl, the Welsh language prevails and can be heard daily on the street. It remains the case that 100% of the indigenous population speak Welsh as a first language. Add to this the fact that the

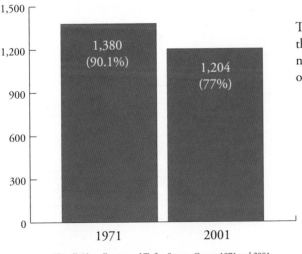

Trends in Welsh in the area of Yr Eifl*; number and percentage of speakers

*Pistyll, Llanaelhaearn and Trefor. Source: Census 1971 and 2001

physical environment has few comparators and it is easy to see why those who identify strongly with Wales' rich cultural environment return to the area time after time.

Is this then some sort of cultural Avalon? What is the real situation facing the Welsh language in the 21st century? Mention has already been made of a decline in overall population in the middle of the last century. This inevitably had an impact on the numbers speaking Welsh in the area albeit the percentages, whilst falling, remained relatively high to the end of the century. Overall, however, as the chart above indicates, there has been a gradual decline in the language in the last 30 years – primarily because of the migration of non-Welsh speakers into the area. Sadly, relatively few – perhaps no more than 2% – make a serious effort and succeed in learning the language of the area they move into. The challenge of integrating in-migrants into the Welsh community remains a real one if the language is to thrive and retain its rightful place as a vibrant national language.

Carl Clowes receiving the RIBA environmental award

Nowhere has there been a more determined attempt to bolster the community and give new vitality than in the area of Yr Eifl. Mention has already been made of the community co-operative Antur Aelhaearn, the first of its kind in the UK. Long before the days of the Welsh Development Agency and economic development departments, the villagers of Llanaelhaearn built their own workshop. Today, with the co-operation of Gwynedd Council, training for 40 young people in skills for the rural environment is provided in the village-owned training centre. The co-operative engendered new confidence in the village and a new lease of life with Llanaelhaearn having a wide range of essential services, second to none in Wales for a population of its size. Other successes such as the village Eisteddfod and the development of a village hall have further empowered the local community. Encouragingly, a new generation of younger people are engaged in promoting their community in a similar way and the language can only benefit as a result.

In Llithfaen a similar story can be said about the community's efforts to help itself. The only tavern in the village closed in the 1980s and, as the village school had closed some 20 years earlier, there was a real danger of the village losing an important place to socialise! The 'Victoria' Inn as it was called remained closed for over a year with no obvious sign of a buyer. With much discussion and an eye for the future, the villagers clubbed together and, with outside support, bought the 'Vic' in yet another co-operative venture. Today 'Tafarn y Fic' as it is now named acts as a regular focus for Welsh entertainment and many of 'Nant's pupils and visitors are able to meet there and speak Welsh with the local community. This degree of symbiosis between the various ventures can only be of benefit to all involved and can and should be developed further.

In 2004, the 'Fic' received a well-deserved capital injection enabling the villagers to develop and expand the original facilities and at the same time provide an important community resource for meetings, entertainment, training etc. When the village shop in Llithfaen closed in the early 1990s, following a series of attempts to run it as a private concern, a similar pattern was adopted. A co-operative venture was again established and, whilst this has proven a very valuable asset for the community, the thin population of the area makes it highly marginal in its viability and its future continues to be of concern for those involved.

The above examples of co-operation, as with Nant Gwrtheyrn, follow an honourable tradition of co-operation in Bro'r Eifl. In Trefor, the village shop, the Co-op and the Clynnog and Trefor bus company or Moto Coch as it is affectionately known locally, both adopted similar examples of co-operation in action. In Trefor, as elsewhere, the same spirit and readiness of the local community to fight its corner for its Welsh identity and viability is self-evident. This is nowhere more so than with Seindorf Arian Trefor, the local brass band which has done much to promote local young musical talent. The cultural tradition of the area is also seen in other fields. Cor Gwrtheyrn (Cerdd Dant traditional Welsh song), Cor Aelwyd Chwilog (young people's choir) and Hogia'r Mynydd (choir) regularly hold concerts in Llŷn and, together with Cwmni Drama Llwyndyrus and their renowned drama productions, contribute extensively to the social life of the neighbouring villages and beyond.

The situation of Welsh at a national level

For many visitors from outside Wales a frequently asked question is what is the situation of the Welsh language today and an honest answer involves some circumspection! Without any doubt a large majority of the population is supportive of the language whether they speak it or not. In a survey by the Welsh Language Board in 2002, 66% of the population said that the future of the language was 'very important' with only 11% saying that the language was of 'no importance'. This expression of goodwill is particularly significant in ensuring that the language thrives.

Following a decline in the fortunes of Welsh throughout last century, the National Census of 2001 showed an increase in the numbers speaking the language in Wales. Some 20.2% of the population spoke Welsh at that time although, according to some less formal surveys, the percentage may be considerably higher – as much as 30%. The difference in percentages may stem from the lack of confidence that many Welsh people have in their

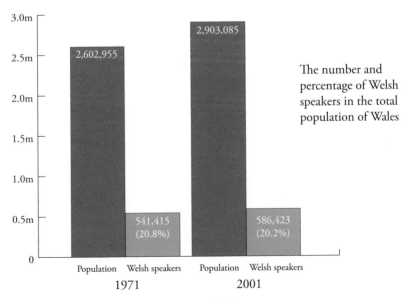

The number and percentage of Welsh speakers in the total population of Wales

Source: Census 1971 and 2001

linguistic capabilities when they complete a government-inspired Census. This lack of confidence can only reflect lack of status and educational policies in the past. The history of the 'Welsh Not' where children speaking Welsh in school were beaten remains in the folk memory for many and others recall how Welsh lacked any status whatsoever until the middle of the last century and remember how, for several centuries previously, it was official policy to rid Wales of the language ('utterly extirp') following the Act of Union of 1536.

The Welsh language, like English, is now compulsory up to the age of 16 years in all state schools in Wales. Research from the Welsh Language Board again shows that the majority of the population support this policy and, according to one study, 78% of the population thought that the education system was the way to 'save the language'. Efforts to promote the Welsh language have to be set in the wider context.

Nant Gwrtheyrn

Ein geiriau sy'n blaguro – yn yr hollt,
Wedi'r hir edwino
Yno'n y gwyll, a hen go'
Y genedl yn egino.

O'r diffwys oer a diffaith – y gwanwyn
A egina obaith;
Drwy ing a rhwd dringa'r iaith
I'r haul a'i sblander eilwaith.

by RJ Rowlands

- There are at least 3,000 languages in the world today

- Already, probably 4,000 languages have disappeared

- The future of any language is less than certain

In 1991, the Fforwm Iaith Genedlaethol (National Language Forum) produced the first comprehensive language strategy for Wales. Today, through the efforts of the Welsh Language Board and latterly the National Assembly for Wales there are policies in place, notably 'Iaith Pawb' which give an enlightened lead to secure its future. More, however, needs to be done and comprehensive legislation which gives full status for the Welsh language in Wales is required.

The private sector, including the major utilities, are currently not covered by legislation and bodies such as the CBI argue against any such moves believing that business would fight shy of Wales if full and equal status with English was implemented. This is a false premise as the Catalan experience clearly illustrates when Catalunya, with powerful language legislation, inspires as one of the major 'motor regions' of Europe. The following points are also worthy of consideration in looking at the future of the Welsh language:

- The world's 14 most frequently used languages are spoken by 60% of the world's population

- A total of just 1 million people speak the world's 500 least common languages

- In April 2004 there were 31 'lesser used languages' in Europe spoken by a total of 31 million people

- Since April 2004 an additional 12 countries have joined the European Union and brought an estimated further 20 languages in a similar situation to the debate

- Each and every one of these minority languages will have problems of 'survival' and identity not dissimilar to Welsh

- There is reason to believe that Welsh is among the world's top 100 most viable languages

It is vitally important therefore that experiences and good practices are exchanged amongst the speakers of the 'lesser used' languages of Europe. Regularly we see visitors to Nant Gwrtheyrn from these regions and small nations and exchange ideas. As Nant Gwrtheyrn grows, so it is hoped that we will see an increase in these exchanges and the development of new and stimulating responses as a result. In this way, a regained confidence in the smaller and often marginalised languages will undoubtedly ensue.

Nant Gwrtheyrn

Tra bo'r byd yn dod â'i blant
i'r Nant i gasglu trysor,
fesul gair o ddydd i ddydd
mi fydd sawl giât yn agor.

by Meirion MacIntyre Huws

Nant Gwrtheyrn today

n reflection, the 1990s were a period of consolidation, some small improvements to the houses and some experimentation with the 'market'. By now, some 25,000 people have had the opportunity to sample the language in the Centre. By way of background, they are very varied! A Nobel Peace Prize winner, an Archbishop and Bishops, Lords, Assembly Members, Members of Parliament, actors, artists, rock groups, heads of corporates and chief civil servants and, as important as anyone, a large number of 'dispossessed' Welsh people, committed to their language and determined to regain it for themselves and their families.

Individuals have come to Nant Gwrtheyrn devoid of any Welsh and left as fluent Welsh speakers. At the same time, many have come from all corners of the world to improve their linguistic skills and experience complete immersion in the Welsh language enabling them to succeed in their task. As a result, many learners have gained the confidence to use Welsh in the workplace. Others have developed sufficient confidence to use it in the media whilst several enlightened alumni, through their leadership role, have been able to introduce supportive policies for the language in their respective organisations.

In the 1990s, there were two significant steps in the life of Wales and its people – the introduction of a new Welsh Language Act in 1993 and the establishment of the National Assembly for Wales in 1997. As a result there was a renewed interest in the language and, as Nant Gwrtheyrn is the only full-time residential centre of its kind, it became important that we responded to the new challenges accordingly.

Re-opening Capel Seilo in 2003 created an opportunity to meet the increased interest from the public for information about the Welsh language and 'Nant's role in the residential teaching of Welsh. Here, within a refurbished chapel, a small-scale interpretation of the area was developed. The limited opportunities afforded, however, created a further stimulus for debate amongst the Trustees. What exactly was the direction the Trust should be taking?

Around the same period, Nant Gwrtheyrn led a marketing initiative which brought together other organisations in the peninsula in common purpose – to try and capture an interest in the casual visitor for a variety of enterprises promoting the best of Welsh culture in the area. As a result, a healthy partnership grew with several key establishments – Ymddiriedolaeth Ynys Enlli (Bardsey Island Trust), Oriel Glyn y Weddw (Art Gallery), Canolfan Ysgrifennu Ty Newydd (Writers' Centre), Plas yn Rhiw (National Trust) and Lloyd George Museum. This partnership can only be beneficial to the economy of the area and will hopefully continue to grow as the important cultural messages reach the visiting population. Taster courses in the Welsh language for tourists have been pioneered by Nant Gwrtheyrn in recent years with great success.

Following the re-opening of Capel Seilo in 2003, there was an increased demand from groups interested in using the Centre either for conferences or as a retreat and the occasional wedding but, paradoxically, we were unable to meet these legitimate demands and maximise the potential, primarily because the access remained problematic and health and safety issues were looming larger day by day. Also, some 25 years since the first re-building project, facilities were beginning to become tired and, in the interim, expectations had changed and new and improved resources were required. The designation of a Graded listing by CADW added to the need to improve the fabric of the village's estate.

So the debate around the future of the 'Nant' intensified! Welsh For Adults had been restructured at an all-Wales level and 'Nant's role clearly had to dovetail into the new and emerging structures as defined by the Welsh Assembly Government. A new economy was required based on an increased level of activity. Enhanced viability, it was argued, would ensue. How to achieve this?

A business case was put forward based on a mixed economy. This would continue to focus on the primary role of a centre teaching 'Welsh to Adults' but would encourage other compatible activities. Two, if not three, varied strands came together in the middle of the decade which were to change the fortunes of 'Nant'. First, Hanson Plc the aggregate company, who owned the adjacent quarry of Porth y Nant were approached about transferring their interests in the quarry to Ymddiriedolaeth Nant Gwrtheyrn. A consultation exercise initiated by the Welsh Assembly Government resulted in the company no longer being able to extract minerals from this area of 'sensitive coastline' and the time was appropriate for the approach. This proved successful and, in 2007, Hanson's interests were transferred to the Trust for a nominal sum. This immediately gave the trustees an opportunity to promote the idea of developing an interpretive role for the granite quarrying industry. Other indigenous interests had such a facility – coal, slate, iron and the woollen industry, so why not granite which had had such an influence on several major cities and been a major source of employment in the area for thousands of men in the early part of last century?

The second factor which influenced the Trustees' course of action, and was to give confidence to the team dedicated to see a viable future for the project, was the gift of a considerable estate by an anonymous benefactor. This gave

The new road to Nant Gwrtheyrn, 2008

the Trustees an important and independent source of funding which would help promote an exciting agenda for the future. 'Nant' has been blessed with a series of gifts and legacies over the years and this in itself has been a continuing source of inspiration for the Trust Board. Now, with a new source of support, we could begin to put our business plan into action.

The third element that was to come into play was a fortuitous combination. The skills and experience of Jim O'Rourke, a consultant employed by the trust, were matched not only with the aspirations of the Trustees with their considerable skills but also with the aspirations of certain key politicians in the One Wales coalition government established following the elections of May 2007. Concerns had been expressed by the Trust for some time about the lack of any serious investment in northern Llŷn and the continued decline of Welsh-speaking communities. Here was a real opportunity for a political input to help meet those aspirations and concerns and make a real contribution to the Government's own policy of revitalising the language as given in Iaith Pawb!

There is little doubt that this area of northern Llŷn, devoid of significant infrastructure and employment, can only benefit from the proposed developments in 'Nant', the first phase of which has now been completed. Major improvements to the access road to Nant Gwrtheyrn were completed in March 2008 and opened by Ieuan Wyn Jones AM, Deputy First Minister for Wales. The new and improved access will facilitate other elements in the business plan – refurbishment and upgrading of the accommodation, new and extended facilities for Caffi Meinir to secure conferences, concerts and weddings and, importantly, new and upgraded facilities for teaching in Y Plas. An important 'entrance' facility to the village – y Porth – will complete the new development and provide a reception, shop and comprehensive interpretive facility for the Centre focusing on the history and development of the Welsh language and the local granite industry. At the time of writing, the specification for large elements of the above is going out to tender.

By now most people can identify with Nant Gwrtheyrn as a location of considerable importance in what was once regarded as an outlandish area with little hope or potential. Many of the obstacles have been overcome and it now

Many windows into the past of the 'Nant' remain

provides an inspiration for those who appreciate the values of Cymru and its population. There is no better location to immerse in the language or to encourage the confidence of learners and the informal nature of support in the local community is an added bonus.

The early ambitions, to see the centre at Nant Gwrtheyrn as an ambassador for, and promoter of, the Welsh language and a creator of local employment are very much to the fore 30 and more years later. Attitudes to the language have, however, changed remarkably in the intervening years. Rarely now is the language vilified and respect grows with each generation as they come to appreciate their heritage more than ever.

Nant Gwrtheyrn has played an important role in that process and the mission for the future is clear – to remain an inspiration and an 'icon' of hope!

Nant Gwrtheyrn

I listen to the echoes
of John Jones crying: 'God
is not good,' and of his wife
correcting him: 'Hush, John.'

'The cuckoo returns
to Gwrtheyrn, contradicting
John Jones, within its voice
bluebells tolling over

the blue sea. There is work
here still, quarrying
for an ancient language
to bring it to the light

from under the years'
dust covering it. Men,
with no palate for fine
words, they helped them down

with their sweat, spitting
them out later in what
served them for prayer. Was
it for this God numbered

their days? Where once pick-
axes would question, now
only the stream ticks, telling
a still time to listeners

at their text-books. Turning
its back on the world,
contemplating without boredom
unchanging horizons this place

knows a truth, for here
is the resurrection
of things. One after one
they arise in answer

to names they are called by,
standing around, shining,
by brief graves from whose hold
willing hands have released them.

By RS Thomas © Kunjana Thomas, 2001